10/18

For Elizabeth, Hilary and Linda, you inspire me.

Black Cats

get a Bad Rap

by J.G. Piper

Illustrated by
Linda Apple

I'm a black cat who crossed paths
with a man in a black hat.

He said I gave him bad luck.

I say things just ran amuck.

I was fast and he was slow.

I even said hello.

I'm a black cat who
got a bad rap.

I'm a black cat who

wore a witch's hat.

They say I was part of a curse.

I say I just got caught in a verse.

I thought she was nice,

we shared a love of mice.

I'm a black cat who

got a bad rap.

I'm a black cat
getting a little shuteye.
No reason to get shaken
and let out a big cry.
I was just a bit sleepy,
not being at all creepy.
I'm a black cat who
got a bad rap.

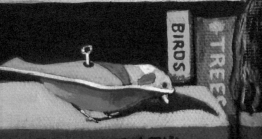

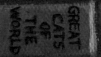

I'm a black cat who

wore a pumpkin as a hat.

I made a boy scream

who was almost a teen.

I was just having fun,

I didn't expect him to run.

I'm a black cat who

got a bad rap.

I'm a black cat who
goes out at night.
I really don't mean
to give you a fright.
I'm friends with the bird and the owl,
I even like the dog
that gives a long howl.
I'm a black cat who
got a bad rap.

We are the **black cats**

traveling from here to **there.**
Our shadows may look spooky
but we're really **unaware.**

We are like black night,
it's just the opposite of day.
Black, it's simply a color,
we truly want to play.
We are the black cats
and we're getting a bad rap.

I'm a black cat who knows

how the wind blows.

It makes sounds of unease

as branches flow in the breeze.

The air may whistle

as I run through the thistle

but it wasn't me who made you flee.

I'm a black cat who

got a bad rap.

I'm a **black cat** who

lays in spun **yarn**.

It's just a cat nap,

don't sound the **alarm**.

You caught me while **cleaning**,

no need to keep **screaming**.

I'm a **black cat** who

got a **bad rap**.

I'm a black cat who
knows a black rat.
He's very subtle
but still gets me in trouble.
We have great fun and clown around,
then get lots of frowns
when we're found uptown.
I'm a black cat who
got a bad rap.

I'm a black cat you can find
near the book rack.
I gave you a chill
as I sat by the window, still.
People think I'm quite magical.
I assure you my intentions
are just casual.
I'm a black cat who
got a bad rap.

MIDNIGHT THE CAT
CAT WHO SAW STARS
WANDS IN THE WILLOWS
MAGICAL FOREST
TANGLED TAILS
MOON, STARS & MAGIC
KETTLES AND CAULDRONS
UNEXPECTED WHISKERS
MYSTICAL SHADOWS
CAT-TASTIC TALES
THE MAGIC MIRROR
ANTIQUE BROOMSTICKS
STAR-CROSSED CATS
WHISKERS
NOTIONS AND POTIONS

I'm a black cat who
      has yellow eyes.
It was Halloween and
      you got surprised.
I meant no harm, was just looking around.
      Sorry your candy dropped to the ground.
I'm a black cat who
      got a bad rap.

We are the **black cats** who enjoy the **night,**
especially when the full moon shines so **bright.**
If you see us on the same night,
as a witch on her **broom**
we ask you not judge quickly
and give us some **room.**

There are certainly some dark stories
    that cast us in bad light.
Consider though, it's the eye of the beholder
    and not black and white.

If you look in your heart, you will see,
    black cats don't deserve a bad rap,
    don't you agree?

Visit us on the web at:
JGPiper.com and AppleArts.com

ISBN-13:
978-0991656103
ISBN-10:
0991656103